Book **1** Easy
Intermediate

Three's A Crowd

These trios can be performed with any other combination of instru

T004085b

Piano accompaniment

plus guitar chords arranged by James Power.

CHESTER MUSIC
London/New York/Paris/Sydney/Copenhagen/Berlin/Madrid/Tokyo

Contents

Exclusive distributors:
Chester Music
(A division of Music Sales Limited)
8/9 Frith Street, London W1D 3JB, England.

Music Sales Corporation
257 Park Avenue South, New York, NY 10010,
United States of America.

Music Sales Pty Limited
120 Rothschild Avenue, Rosebery, NSW 2018, Australia.

Order No. PM178605R
ISBN 0-7119-9375-0
This book © Copyright 2002 Chester Music
The instruments featured on the cover are provided by
Macari's Musical Instruments, London.
Models provided by Truly Scrumptious and Norrie Carr.
Photography by George Taylor.
Cover design by Chloë Alexander.
Printed in the United Kingdom.

Swan Lake

Music by Peter Ilyich Tchaikovsky
(1840 - 1893)

3

Country Garden

Traditional Folk Dance

The Happy Farmer

Music by Robert Schumann
(1810 - 1856)

Minuet

Music by Ludwig Van Beethoven
(1770 - 1827)

Cutie Flootie

Music by James Power

Morning Has Broken

Words by Eleanor Farjeon, Music Traditional

Irish Washerwoman

Irish Folk Song

Lincolnshire Poacher

Traditional

The Kerry Dance

Molloy/Traditional

When The Saints Go Marching In

Words by Katherine Purvis, Music by James Milton Black

The Wild Horseman

Music by Robert Schumann
(1810 - 1856)

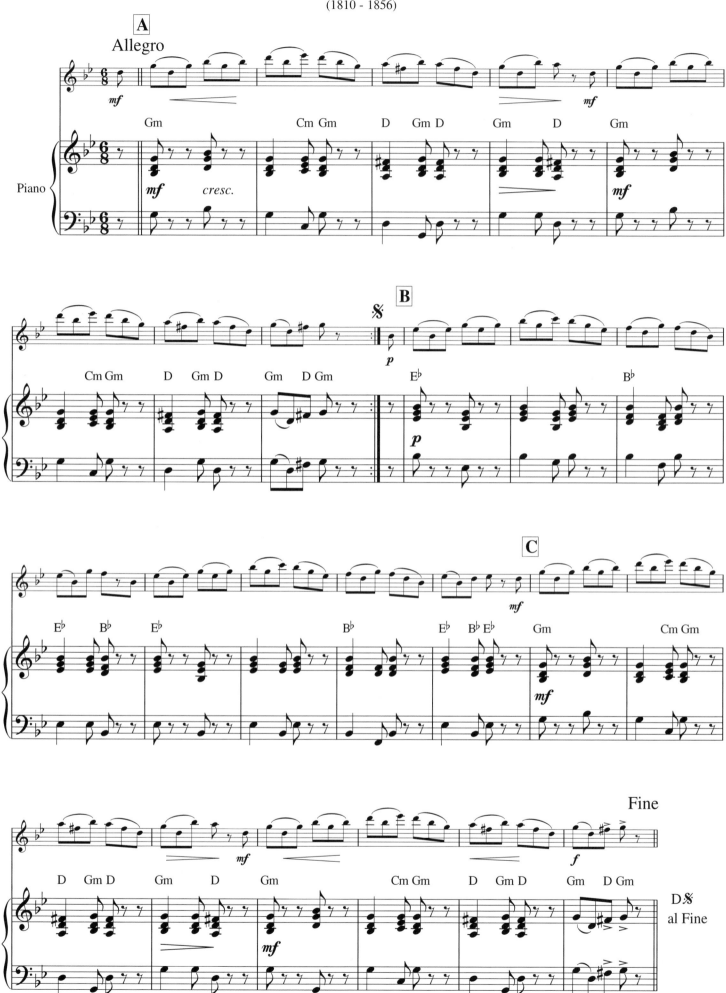

Jingle Bells

Words & Music by J.S. Pierpont

God Rest Ye Merry, Gentlemen

Traditional

20

Sailors' Hornpipe

Traditional

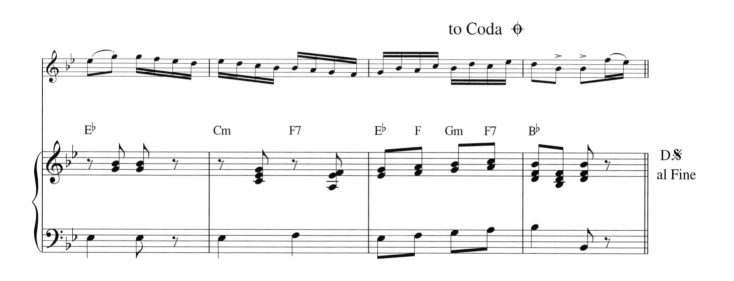

23

Mexican Hat Dance

Traditional

24

Phil The Fluter

Irish Traditional

26

Humoresque

Music by Dvořák
(1841 - 1904)

Allegro *from* Sonata in C major K545

Music by Wolfgang Amadeus Mozart

(1756 - 1791)

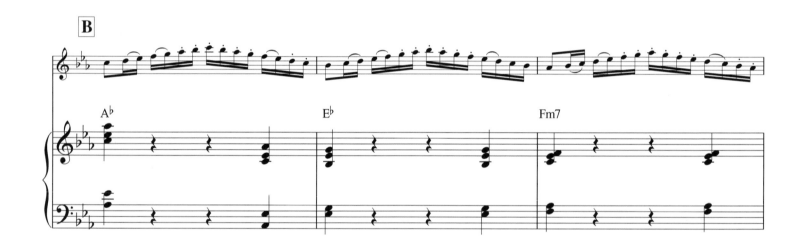

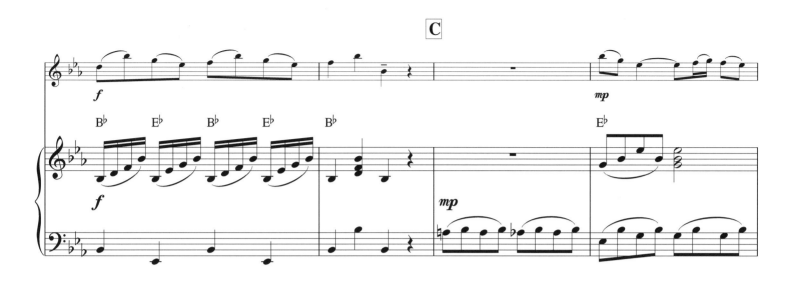

Scheherezade

Music by Rimsky-Korsakov
(1844 - 1908)